our own beautiful brutality

poems by

Karen Poppy

Finishing Line Press
Georgetown, Kentucky

our own beautiful brutality

Copyright © 2021 by Karen Poppy
ISBN 978-1-64662-543-7 First Edition
All rights reserved under International and Pan-American Copyright Conventions. No part of this book may be reproduced in any manner whatsoever without written permission from the publisher, except in the case of brief quotations embodied in critical articles and reviews.

ACKNOWLEDGMENTS

I am grateful to the editors of the following journals, in which the poems in this book first appeared, or are soon forthcoming:

The American Journal of Poetry: "The How-to Guide of Giant Sable Antelope (*Hippotragus niger variani*)"
Golden Walkman: "Hineni"
Peregrine: "Bounce"
Queen Mob's Teahouse: "Upper Antelope Canyon"
Seventh Quarry: "You Tell Me of Stars" and "Cats versus Antelopes"
Sinister Wisdom: "Diving at the Lip of the Water"
Swimming with Elephants: "Treehouse on Mars"

Publisher: Leah Huete de Maines
Editor: Christen Kincaid
Cover Art: Lydia Lee, photographer; Sherry Gilbert, photo art/design
Author Photo: Lorelei Ghanizadeh Voorsanger
Cover Design: Elizabeth Maines McCleavy

Order online: www.finishinglinepress.com
also available on amazon.com

Author inquiries and mail orders:
Finishing Line Press
PO Box 1626
Georgetown, Kentucky 40324
USA

Table of Contents

Matriarchy 1

The How-to Guide of Giant Sable Antelope
  (*Hippotragus niger variani*) 2

By the Bridge, by the River 5

You Tell Me of Stars 7

Bounce 8

Climbing Boy 9

Upper Antelope Canyon 11

The Nobleman Harnath of Khimsar, with an Indian Antelope
  in an Alternate Universe 12

Postcard to Jussuf, the Prince of Thebes 13

Small Antelope 14

Diving at the Lip of the Water 15

Desire of Touch 20

Cautionary Figure of a Species in Decline 21

Cats versus Antelopes 22

Hineni 23

Treehouse on Mars 26

Notes 29

Matriarchy
How was my life—through yours—made mine?

Sometimes, every day, several times a day actually,
I'm lonely for you, your exaggerated movements,
Your voice in deep register, your compact majesty.

Sometimes, every day, several times a day actually,
I'm angry at you, the richness and poverty
Of this gift. Your voice and body, my legacy.

At the end of life, Sable leader passes matriarchy
To one female in the group, who takes on her traits.
That female becomes dark and bold, more like a male.

She becomes exactly like the passing matriarch,
Although no one knows how, whether pheromones
Or fate. How in sudden shift did I become you?

Your eyes flashed and turned the way their minds do,
Toward any perceived threat, however innocent.
Unable to retract my words, I suffered greatly.

My mind pricked and turned the way their ears do,
Toward the most important. Pricked and turned,
Wanting some remnant of you, wanting our story.

For nothing is more painful than becoming,
Than knowing, the hard learning registered.
The regret and anguished gratefulness, forever.

I felt the change even then, the moment over.
How I laughed at you and said nothing.
How you laughed at me and interred

A twig with your shoe. A burial, a planting.

The How-to Guide of Giant Sable Antelope
(Hippotragus niger variani)

Part I.

How to survive, avoid extinction:
Be revered, prized for distinct beauty.
How to die, become extinct:
Be revered, prized for distinct beauty.

They will work to save us.
They will work to hunt us.
Humans, they do both and
Call it worship, call it love.

Humans have this facial expression
They call a smile.
Show their teeth
With which many eat meat.

A smile gives the human face
That special glow,
Like when sunlight glints
Off our long, majestic horns.

We drop to our knees.
It seems like surrender.
Then our horns cut
Animal who saw us as prey.

We've been known to—
Like other Sables—
Impale the lion,
The crocodile,
Creatures who smile.

Part II.

Don't take us lightly.
We survived, the very few.
Humans call our status
Critically endangered,
Startled that we still exist.

We are startled that they still exist.
These humans, as they call themselves.

They call us Giant Sable Antelope
In their various languages.
Hippotragus niger variani
In a language less endangered
Than we, but they call it dead.

We call ourselves, each other.
By lock of our horns.
By look that warns
Of small wild dog,
Great predator.

Our past generations long ago
Gathered in vast groups
At and near cool quench
Of water, leafy nourishment.
We lived in our own beautiful brutality.

We and humans could still live like that.
Angry aggressors who fight selectively.

Fighting, mating, and yes—dying.
Nature coursed, a wide river,
Rife with life and danger.
Then humans began over-killing,
Hunting more and more.

Hunted us. Hunted each other,
In and after civil war.
Angola, our only home, and
For many humans, theirs.
Devastation dried up our rivers.

Our numbers, near extinction.
Humans died too, suffered
So much lost life. More than 500,000.
Over one million human beings displaced.
In-fighting after liberation.

Even as they war, kill in sport,
Humans, they live in large
Population, warp and weft
The weave of all of earth's
Existence, all of creation.

We cannot trust them.

By the Bridge, by the River

Before the blast,
I saw his great
Horns, though
No one would
Believe me.

Their wide
Arc smashed,
Many starred
Explosion,
Scars against
My vision.

A divine sight,
When I first
Spotted him,
Bold within
Tall grasses.

Then I bent
Down among
Wildflowers
And rushes.
By the bridge,
By the river.

What I found,
Just as rare.
Something
I had long
Prayed for:
A real toy.

A metal tin,
Treasure box.
I tried then to
Loosen its mud
Seal with stick,
Hit it hard
Against rock.

Bomb, not
Treasure box.
My hands, face
Ripped apart.
My eyes,
Blinded.

My mind now
Sees flashes.
The stars
Of fractured
Antelope horns.
My own survival.

You Tell Me of Stars

You tell me of stars.
How they chase you,
Shining like great claws, he
White-teethed and holding
You down in the dark.

Your father unbuckles his belt.
You, as small as a mouse,
Still-gripped with fear,
Although they call you
Red deer, celestial doe.

You tell me of your blood
Dripping to sea, becoming
Islands of enveloped sunset.
You tell me of your transformation.
Deer to antelope, scorpion's poison.

You tell me, and I tell you:
He must be brought down
Before he kills all animals,
Before he violates the entire earth—
But whatever we do, he stalks you, his daughter, forever.

Bounce

Between 10% and 14% of married women will be raped at some point during their marriages.
        —Statistic provided on National Coalition Against Domestic Violence (NCADV) website

When I said no, he
Woke me every hour.
Demanded to bounce,
Rode me like a horse.

(The way the cruel,
The ignorant ride—
Insisting, not asking.
Breaking and raging.)

It killed me, you know.
Bruised ribs, torn inside.
Also, a slow soul death.
So imagine his surprise

When this dead thing—
Mounted and stuffed—
Came back to life and left.

Decided to bounce.

Climbing Boy

Small-flamed flowers, buried in ash,
Smoking embers fallen through grate.
Evening's fire not fully extinguished,
But almost—a short, suffocated life.

That mantle over nursery fireplace,
I'll never forget. Or child sleeping there
By candlelight. Gentle, dimpled face.
Maybe two years younger than me.

At five, the orphanage gave me to Jim.
To sweep chimneys, a climbing boy—
Rising as if to Heaven, a skinny stem—
Able to root and rise in darkness.

By candlelight, the boy slept sweet.
By candle flame, higher I climbed.
Billy below burned my bare feet.
"This'll make you dance faster!"

Up I went, into such dark with your mind
You see: white sheet tucked close to his cheek
By someone's rosy hand, plump and kind.
Mantle tiles alive in a living green.

Mantle tiles sculpted with beautiful creatures.
Almost like tiny horses with double horns.
Painted gold against the green, features
In high relief, detailed. I remember my wonder.

I climbed and climbed, thinking of them,
Gathering soot in my bag, gathering soot
On every inch of my naked skin, my skin
Bloodied, rubbed rough by brick and stone.

Billy behind, too far down now to burn
My feet. Even flayed, I felt good, alone.
Soot cleansed my every sting. I would learn
To love its cleansing, pretend against all pain.

A few days later, Jim began to beat and bugger me.
Did the same to Billy, and Billy sometimes cried,
Soot washed to salty pink. I tried not to cry.
I became tough as my skin, torn and torn again.

My dead parents, Billy, I will see them in full light.
In Heaven, and in current time, so very soon.
The gentry child sleeping there that night,
My first chimney cleaned, he's now a man.

Seventeen years—me, first chimney boy then finally
Devil Jim died. I became my own man, Master Sweep.
With what I have, Dr. Pott told me any month or day.
He looked at me with such blind pity, but he forgets:

A chimney sweep is lucky.

Upper Antelope Canyon

Light shafted womb,
        Fire flood
    Each layer.
                             Striature,
              Curved flexure.
                              Muted ocean.
        Emptied chamber.
Muscled sweep of sand   and sandstone.
                      Stillness after.
Coolness within heat.
                      Nothing the same, except
In its essential.
                Beam hits one spot or several.
Celestial tumble
                in one imperceptible
Inhale, exhale.
        Brings us
                to important meditation.
What do these lunged branches breathe but a blaze,
    Surged through
           Incandescent structure?
Our mighty wonder cracks open its delicate shell.
    Glow, an expansion, tawny to indigo.
No one listens more intently, or
            With more intention,
    Than to sounds of their own mortality,
But silence tells us more.

The Nobleman Harnath of Khimsar,
with an Indian Antelope in an Alternate Universe

This antelope, half my size,
But for his great horns,
Taught me to consider
Compassion and learn it.
Also, patience, self-restraint,
Forbearance and mercy
Through the long study of
His large, amber eyes.
Yes, and love. Even as
I looked into my own
Reflection stated there,
I felt deep love for him,
Gave up the hunt, let
Him graze from my hand.

Before, when he served to
Lure and drive hidden game
From their dark, leafy cover
Toward me and my huntsmen,
I bestowed upon him a fine
Crimson collar with bells.
Bells that rang compassion.
Yes, compassion, patience,
Self-restraint, forbearance,
Mercy, and love for all to
Hear. Bells that remind me
To keep my sword sheathed
At my side and his instinct
In front of me, melding into
My intuition. Wisdom rung
Like his bells. Cerulean,
Golden-sweet reverberations.
Gods and goddesses singing,
Their skin and sky, blue, gilded.

Postcard to Jussuf, the Prince of Thebes
When you say that you have no road anymore, only ravines.

Sometimes blood and sky
Must merge to complete
The picture. Sometimes
Rock and animal compete
In proud silence, meticulous
Stillness of muted moss,
Naked, ever-moving stream.

Sometimes brush and paint
Join ideas and flesh, curve
A fluted, musical course,
A galloped vision of flight.
Illuminated image, bright
Expression, not distortion.
Lilac pools over black, green.

When I send it to you, small
Offering, every hatch of paint
A kiss from your Blue Rider,
Hooves of this persistent antelope
Ghostly hidden behind stone,
Behind him, facing sea, my horse.
You, my Prince, are never alone.

Small Antelope

I call to you, in full fleet run,
As if I mean to escape you.
As if my gallop is fear, and fear
It is. I am afraid, but
I seek you, dare you to chase me.

When I embark on high seas,
Tie me to a mast. Like Odysseus,
Near-wrecked by wild song.
Or like a willing martyr,
Trembling there. Small antelope,
Shivering in last breaths,
Mortal wounds of arrows.

I want to submit to you,
Beautiful storm, beautiful man.
Like a trembling antelope, dying
In the beauty of poetry.
Your fingers and lips and eyes,
Sweet arrows released from quiver.
My flesh, pierced and quivering.

I also want to be each arrow,
Surrendering my point, surrendering
My point in that point, trembling,
Heaving in that point called death.
Silver apples, mirrored moons, you
My perfect, fast-paced twin.
My fronds bed down in your cool moss.

¡Ay amor, ay dios! In that truth
At last. Deserving to be loved.

Diving at the Lip of the Water
for Rachel

I am the wall at the lip of the water
I am the rock that refused to be battered
I am the dyke in the matter, the other
I am the wall with the womanly swagger
I am the dragon, the dangerous dagger
I am the bulldyke, the bulldagger

From "She Who," by Judy Grahn, at the beginning of Chapter Six of her book, *Another Mother Tongue*, about the linguistic history of the word *bulldyke/bulldike*.

The common duiker [a small antelope, name pronounced dyker] *uses a pair of glands under its eyes for scent marking with a tarry secretion. Duikers run with a distinctive darting and diving style when they flee danger. This gives rise to its common name which is the Africaans for "diver."*

From the website of *Fascinating Africa*.

Between trees, within edges
Of forests, woodlands.
Among open clearings.
With scent markings below eyes,
We label another our own.

This is how we bull duikers do it.
We males secrete a substance,
Deftly labeling, marking with
Our tarry, leaf-scented names,
Our territories, calves, mates.

When we run, we dive at the lip
Of the water, be it a field, a deep
Forest, a body. We do this from love
Or fear—which you understand,
For you and I mark in the same way.

Humans cover with other scents,
Afraid of labels or diving into them.
Each marking, energy, power.
Labels we give ourselves,
Labels we use to mark another.

Some names change in meaning,
Mutate over time, original markers
Lost. Some we mistake in origin:
Bull duiker, a male antelope.
Never the origin of bulldyke.

We cull meaning from sound,
Just as our eyes tell us what
We see. We feel. An energy,
A power. You misread her,
By mistake or by design.

We can only guess at origin
Of bulldyke and bulldagger.
Roman times. Harlem Renaissance
Novels. Women singing the Blues.
Dig within erasure and resistance.

I like the Blues best, the song
Written and sung by Bessie
Jackson (pseudonym of Lucille
Bogan)—explicit and raw,
Prophetic dirty Blues, peel

Back the layers, and here
It is, lay of the land. Women
Can be whatever they choose:
Comin' a time, B.D. women
Ain't gonna need no men.

"Bulldike is the kind of word
Most women hope to avoid
All their lives, for few things
Are more horrifying to be called,"
But these women hold the dagger.

Surrounded by hostile bulls.
Sometimes surrounded by
Women afraid of difference.
Sometimes by people who
Insist that she must be a man.

We can reclaim the name
"Used on a woman like a whip."
We can reclaim our own swagger.
Our own swagger can be womanly.
Our swagger can mark our love.

So says my lover, who loves me
Body and soul. There must be
Space for everyone. For women
Who swagger. For all women.
Don't say she isn't lesbian because

She loves me. There must be space
For her. For me: queer, never quite
Within borders, between, on edges,
In the open. I want to make that clear.
Embrace and don't isolate us.

Surround us with love, define us,
Mark us by our love for each other.
I love a woman, but my gender bleeds
Beyond labels and markings, no matter
What I'm called, and what you call me.

No matter what I call myself, I am marked.
I bleed monthly. I've been attacked with
Thrown stones, called a dyke. I swagger
Womanly, and I love a woman, but
I am not one. I swagger, and I shift.

We have to love each other.
Those on either side of gender
Binary. Those who transform,
Transgress—and those who
Stay hidden in heavy cover.

Also those like me,
Who don't fit evenly,
Who shift and move
Without gender, and
Within sexuality.

Some things, especially hate,
Can mark you. They have
Marked me. Call me what
You will. I love you,
As I do, unconditionally.

I will love my lover,
Knowing her beauty
Shakes the earth, comes
From another place, full
Of energy, power.

The sleek duiker dives
In escaping run, zig zags
Like my lover's tongue—
But my lover is not afraid.
My body a safe field, a sheltering forest.

She cleanses me, recitations
Of sacred ash, this beautiful
Burning, a pooled release.
When I cry, I am hers, and
I am her. She holds me.

There lived a warrior queen named
Boudica. Bulldike, or bulldiker.
In a last stand, with warrior daughters,
Boudica burned Londinium,
Now modern London, to the ground.

She led a vast uprising when Romans
Invaded to destroy her people.
What happens if we erase her name?
What happens to our own markings
Of energy, power? Let her be named.

Let us dive at the lip of the water,
Into love, and fearless. Let us
Mark each other with freedom,
Like bold Boudica at the helm
Of the chariot, horses charging—

No one holding the reins.

Desire of Touch

A milky edge, light
In her eyes, liquid
Bloom, opalescence.

Their look touches
With reflection of
Watered brilliance,
Sun wading through
Night silk and stars.

Although I judge her
Look by what it says:
Lens a mirror
For every object, every
Thought of living grass.

Soon to caress her lips
With green wonderment.
Crave to graze, desire
Of touch, like
Sunlight, moonlight,
Through fingertips.

Cautionary Figure of a Species in Decline

Someone will recognize me
As an animal caught
In crosshairs of history,
But not remembered or taught.

A creature whose rhyme
Is wraith language of shadow,
A hoofed quatrain whose time
Is gone by tomorrow.

Yet, some wisp of me remains
In rain-drenched forest,
In light upon lichens.
Past and present, chorused.

Will this be enough to warn?
Body from spirit, a couplet torn.

Cats versus Antelopes

Now it was my turn to smile faintly. I was not going to let anyone—not even the British poet from St. Louis—spoil my Literary Evening.
   —Groucho Marx, in a June 1964 letter to his brother, Gummo, regarding dinner in London with his pen pal, T.S. Eliot

Antelopes move
Composed,
Lyrically.

I am the antelope,
The poet, returned
To the field.

Before you, I bow
My great horns,
Never obsequiously.

Then I run you through
With the most
Magnificent part of me.

Your cons, always greater
Than your prose, but
I still love the cats.

Hineni

He walks hesitantly, though pushed, driven.
        The desert of his exile.
Hineni. Here I am. On his head, our every sin.

The scapegoat, like God, is everywhere,
        Omnipresent.
Even in our fast. Even in his dying animal thirst.

Hineni he'ani mima'as. Here I am, poor in deeds.
        Our cantor sings.
We still atone through another, our voices dry.

Cantor, shofar, ancient goat silent and alone.
        Sound and silence
Cross through time, a reverberating civil war.

Sound and silence. *Hineni.* I walk hesitantly,
        Like that goat, through
Our transgressions. Sound on my head, silently.

I want voice to fill me. I think of every war,
        Every war zone.
I think of the times that I have said nothing.

Thousands die in sound and silence
        Of civil war.
I have said nothing. The news speaks

Its black ink like hoofprints soon
        Swept by
Immortal desert, bleached to white bone.

Yemen, in civil war. Thousands killed.
        Far away,
And look what they've done to the Jews.

Less than 100 remain in Yemen, those few
        Nearing extinction.
Hunted and murdered, driven out, in exile.

Like living scapegoat, herded to survival.
        Now in Israel, America,
The diaspora. Less than 100 Jews remain in Yemen.

I think of that number again. Of thousands, millions
        Against whom civil war
Does not discriminate. Wounded, killed. Civilians.

Hineni, but can I speak for them? Those few Jews,
        Those millions of civilians?
The rubble of humanity since Solomon kissed

Sheba, his inner garden luxurious and sun-washed.
        Wisdom comes from within.
I let another speak for me, but I learn my own wisdom.

Mine dark, in silence of congregation, the singular voice
        Begging atonement.
Knowing a child bleeds, knowing a mother starves.

Knowing disease swarms over crumbling walls, bombards.
        Knowing every war is our war.
Every child, our child. Every mother, our mother.

Here I am, within the singular voice, not singular.
        Here I am. *Hineni*.
The shofar that sounds today, Yom Kippur.

Here I am. *Hineni*. Every silence, every sound,
        Every war. Here I am.
The scapegoat, the singer, the loud-blasted shofar.

Not only ram's horn, but yes, the shofar of the Yemeni.
    Kudu antelope horn,
This shofar shakes the heart with terrifying beauty.

Luminous as Solomon's kiss, the time from which
    Yemeni Jews may
Possibly trace their origin. Here I am. *Hineni.*

We are broken pottery, silence, and strident sound.
    We are alchemy
Of a changing life. Our words, our deeds—O God,

                  For all of us. Have mercy.

Treehouse on Mars

When we're born, and old enough,
We'll build a treehouse
On Mars, just
Like one we heard
Our parents' parents built
To play in as children on Earth.

Our Martian colony
Will have no trees.
Only small plants
For consumption.
No birds singing in branches.
No sun shining through leaves.

We'll build our treehouse,
Not in a tree, but on
An artificial resin trunk.
Ancient song of birds
Will filter in from speakers.
Pink glow will light our days.

When we're born, and old enough,
We will learn of trees.
How they lived and
Burned with finality in
Forests and jungles
Of memory and loss.

New trees never could
Meaningfully replace
Old-growth in locations
Strange on our tongues:
Uganda, Kenya, California,
Tongass, Siberia, Indonesia.

When we're born, and old enough,
We'll live on a planet
Far from scent of real resin, pine.
Far from sound of wind through woods.
Far from shade of towering canopies.
Far from trees' majestic heights.

Never will we have memory
Of vast Amazonian wonders,
Jungle animals, forest animals.
Just pictures, holograms, stored DNA.
Koala, Orangutan, Giraffe,
Lion, Antelope, Gazelle.

When we're born, and old enough,
We'll live here, born here
Like our parents.
Tell stories in secret
Of how we want to
Rebuild Earth.

Although we'll know, like
Our treehouse, our dream
Is not real, and never can be.
The trees and animals, gone.
No matter what we've kept,
What we've stored.

At this point, even our own
Existence is hypothetical,
Since life on Mars cannot
Likely occur, be sustained.
Right now, humans have to start
By trying to save Earth.

As we say what we fear,
Our voices stay stuck, unheard
In a distant, probably
Impossible future,
Like roots dead or never born:
It is too late. Too much is lost.

No. Humans must do everything now—
Make sure this never comes true.
Take care of Earth, and each other.

Notes

"Matriarchy" is inspired by information from the B. Bryan Preserve in Point Arena, California regarding how the Sable Antelope matriarch passes on leadership at the end of life to a female in the herd, and that female then takes on the matriarch's traits, including physical ones. The new matriarch becomes like the dying matriarch, darker and bolder. A leader.

"The How-to Guide of Giant Sable Antelope (*Hippotragus niger variani*)" draws from the blog of Pedro Vaz Pinto, who re-discovered the Palanca Negra Gigante after Angola's almost three decades-long civil war: https://angolafieldgroup.com/palanca-negra.

"By the bridge, by the River" is a fictional account, inspired by the real-life story of Minga, a young girl in Angola who mistakenly played with an explosive device (http://legacyofwar.com/scars-forgotten-war-legacy-landmines-angola/). The Giant Sable Antelope is the national symbol of Angola, considered sacred and treasured. It is critically endangered, following Angola's almost three decade long civil war. I dedicate this poem to Minga, who learned braille and wants to be a teacher, and to the Giant Sable Antelope. Landmines remain a tragic post-war legacy in Angola and so many other nations, with people blinded, maimed, and killed by them—including children. Landmines also injure and kill animals.

"You Tell Me of Stars" came into being after reading Robert Bringhurst's final movement of "New World Suite No. 3," "IV: Winter Solstice, Cariboo Mountains": "Orion, the old god, disguised as a deer, is out /stalking Aldebaran, the doe, his daughter, forever."

"Bounce" broaches the topic of marital rape. While the statistic cited at the beginning of the poem indicates the percentage of women who will be raped during marriage, the statistic is not inclusive of other genders and gender identities. Marital rape is unfortunately perpetrated against women, as well as people of other genders and gender identities.

"Climbing Boy" is inspired by the sad history of chimney sweeps, with children used for this labor due to their small size and agility. In 1775, Percivall Pott, an English surgeon, discovered the first known occupationally caused cancer, scrotal cancer in chimney sweeps. His discovery helped to bring about the Chimney Sweepers Act 1788.

"Upper Antelope Canyon" is about the slot canyon of that name, located on Navajo land east of Page, Arizona. The Navajo call this canyon *Tsé bighánílíní*, "the place where water runs through rocks." Antelope are not among the wildlife here, despite the canyon's name in English. While the canyon in English is called Upper Antelope Canyon, and its companion canyon is called Lower Antelope Canyon, this name derives from the population of pronghorn that once lived in the area. Pronghorn are often referred to as antelope, and its Latin name, *Antilocapra americana*, means "American goat-antelope." It is, however, not a member of the goat or the antelope family, and is not related to African antelopes.

"The Nobleman Harnath of Khimsar, with an Indian Antelope in an Alternate Universe" draws inspiration from a miniature painting located in the Asian Art Museum in San Francisco: http://onlinecollection.asianart.org/view/objects/asitem/origin@Rajasthan%20state/140?t:state:flow=c4736345-d808-4084-9111-11e1108c7212.

"Postcard to Jussuf, the Prince of Thebes" draws from these sources:
    1. Jewish German poet and playwright Else Lasker-Schüler (February 11, 1869—January 22, 1945) introduced herself in a letter on November 9, 1912 to Expressionist painter and printmaker Franz Marc (February 8, 1880—March 4, 1916): "I am Jussuf the Prince of Thebes." He sent her dozens of postcards with his paintings, including one of an antelope, as well as one with an antelope and a deer. The postcard with the painting of the solitary antelope has a message from Marc as to the sad news of his father's death. [Franz Marc: Postcards to Prince Jussuf, translated by Peter-Klaus Schuster, Prestel, 1988.]
    2. In her first letter to Marc, responding to Marc's woodcut

illustration of her poem "Versöhnung" ("Reconciliation" or "Atonement"), she wrote:

> Wertester Mahler,
>
> Wenn ich nach München komme, (Ich bin Jussuf der Prinz von Theben) soll ich Franz Marc besuchen? Die blauen Reiter schenken mir dann eine Stunde und ich bringen Ihnen bunte Steine mit. Ich habe viele Gedichte gedichtet, auch die Versöhnung—warum haben Sie die Versöhnung gezeichnet—sind sie auch so schmerzlich verloren wie ich, dass ich keinen Weg mehr habe nur Schluchten.

> Esteemed Painter,
>
> When I come to Munich, (I am Jussuf the Prince of Thebes) should I visit Franz Marc? The blue rider will then give me a moment and I will bring him colorful stones. I have written many poems, among them Versöhnung—Why did you illustrate Versöhnung—are you also painfully lost as I am, that I have no road anymore, only ravines.

[https://web.stanford.edu/group/berlin/data2/naama_3_26/sturm_correspondence.html, citing to:
Else Lasker-Schüler/ Franz Marc Mein lieber, wundervoller, blauer Reiter: Privater Briefwechsel, Herausgegeben von Ulrike Marquart und Heinz Röllecke, Artemis & Winkler, Düsseldorf, 1998.

Der Deutsche Expressionismus: Formen und Gestalten, Herausgegeben von Hans Steffen, Vandenhoeck & Ruprecht, Göttingen, 1965.]

"Small Antelope" is inspired by the letter Federico García Lorca wrote to Carlos Morla Lynch before leaving Madrid for Paris, and then on to the United States and Cuba: "Tengo además un gran deseo de escribir, un amor irrefrenable por la poesía, por el verso puro que llena mi alma todavía estremecida como un pequeño antílope por las últimas brutales flechas. Pero...¡adelante! Por muy humilde que yo sea, creo que merezco ser amado." "I have, moreover, a great desire to write, an unbridled love for poetry, for the pure verse that fills my soul, still trembling like a small antelope from the last brutal arrows. But...onward! As humble as I may be, I deserve to be loved." I believe in his letter, he likely meant that he deserved to be loved by people reading his poetry abroad, but I hope he also knew that he deserved romantic love.

"Diving at the Lip of the Water" delves into the possible origins of the terms "bull dyke" and "bull dagger," and the reclaiming/reframing of these words as powerful ones. This poem quotes from Judy Grahn's book, *Another Mother Tongue*, as well as Bessie Jackson's "B.D. Woman's Blues."

"Desire of Touch" draws from the imagery and symbolism of the Arabian Oryx, thought to be the source of the unicorn legend.

"Cautionary Figure of a Species in Decline" is a sonnet in the voice of an antelope whose species is being driven to extinction.

"Cats versus Antelopes," is about the seemingly tension-laden correspondence between Groucho Marx (Jewish comedian, not formally educated) and T.S. Eliot (notoriously anti-Semitic, lauded poet). Both men admired each other, but reading between the lines, one biographer has posited that they had a strained relationship in their letters: https://www.newyorker.com/books/page-turner/the-fraught-friendship-of-t-s-eliot-and-groucho-marx. After T.S. Eliot passed away, Valerie Eliot made a very lucrative decision: she allowed Andrew Lloyd Webber to use *Old Possum's Book of Practical Cats* for his musical, "Cats." Maybe Groucho Marx rubbed off on Valerie Eliot, and maybe Groucho Marx is having one more laugh as the current version of "Cats" (the 2019 movie) is roundly panned.

"Hineni" draws from the following sources:

1. https://dbs.bh.org.il/place/yemen (a. "The origin story of the Jewish settlement in Yemen has many versions. One of them draws upon the famous romance in the biblical Book of Kings between King Solomon and the Queen of Sheba, who is believed to have ruled in ancient Yemen. According to this version, the Jewish community of Yemen existed as far back as the 10th century BCE." b. "The term 'scapegoat' originates from the goat sent out in biblical times by the High Priest on Yom Kippur to die in the desert, after the High Priest had confessed the sins of the people and transferred them onto its head. Time went by, the Temple was destroyed, the Jews scattered all over the world—and ironically they themselves became the scapegoat to other nations, especially in times of political instability." and c. Information about the modern-day exodus of Yemeni Jews to Israel.)

2. https://www.hrw.org/world-report/2019/country-chapters/yemen ("The armed conflict in Yemen has killed and injured thousands of Yemeni civilians since it began. As of November 2018, 6,872 civilians had been killed and 10,768 wounded, the majority by Saudi Arabia-led coalition airstrikes, according to the Office of the United Nations High Commissioner for Human Rights (OHCHR). The actual civilian casualties are likely much higher. Thousands more have been displaced by the fighting and millions suffer from shortages of food and medical care.")

3. https://www.nytimes.com/2015/02/19/world/middleeast/persecution-defines-life-for-yemens-few-jews.html ("The last of Yemen's once numerous Jews, who predated Muslims by many centuries, have seldom been so threatened and had so few protectors. The Houthis, who now dominate the country, are particularly strong in the two places with confirmed remaining Yemeni Jews: here in Raida, where there are 55 Jews, and in Sana, the capital, where a small number live under what amounts to house arrest by the Houthi leadership."

4. The poem, "Sheba's Hesitation," by Rumi for the image of Solomon having, as Rumi writes, "a beautiful garden inside himself." Also, Rumi's poem "Solomon to Sheba" for these inspirational words:

"The alchemy/of a changing life is the only truth." [Translation by Coleman Barks with John Moyne])

"Treehouse on Mars" tells us what we already know: we have to save Earth, if possible, from climate change, human wars, and other factors that are destroying our planet.

Karen Poppy has work published in *The Cortland Review* (Best of the Net nomination), *Naugatuck River Review* (11th Annual Narrative Poetry Contest Finalist), *The Gay and Lesbian Review Worldwide, ArLiJo,* and *Wallace Stevens Journal,* as well as in various anthologies and other publications. Her chapbook, *CRACK OPEN/ EMERGENCY,* is published by Finishing Line Press (2020), and her chapbook, *EVERY POSSIBLE THING,* is published by Homestead Lighthouse Press (2020).

Her poems, "Austria by Train" and "Walt Whitman Celebrates Himself," are included under Holocaust Poetry in the United States Holocaust Memorial Museum Library and Archives in Washington D.C. Karen Poppy's poem, "The Aisle Not Taken," has been chosen by the 22nd Poet Laureate of the United States, Tracy K. Smith, to read on her national radio show and podcast, The Slowdown. Two of her poems, "Which to Prefer" and "A Horse Sees Things Differently" made it to the quarterfinal stages of the 2018 Able Write Prize for Poetry. A group of her poems have been shortlisted by *The Raw Art Review* for their 2018 Walt Whitman Prize for Poetry. Other of her poems have been longlisted for the 2018 American Literary Review Contest for Poetry.

Karen Poppy is an attorney licensed in California and Texas. She lives in the San Francisco Bay Area.

www.ingramcontent.com/pod-product-compliance
Lightning Source LLC
LaVergne TN
LVHW041505070426
835507LV00012B/1346